D0888224

BODY
CHANGES

Joely Carey

BODY
CHANGES

Joely Carey

BARRON'S

First edition for the United States, its territories and dependencies,
and Canada published in 2002 by Barron's Educational Series, Inc.

Conceived and created by
Axis Publishing Limited
8c Accommodation Road
London NW11 8ED
www.axispublishing.co.uk

Creative Director: Siân Keogh
Designer: Juliet Brown
Project Editor: Charlotte Stock
Production Manager: Sue Bayliss

NOTE
The opinions and advice expressed in this book are intended as a guide only.
The publisher and author accept no responsibility for any injury or loss
sustained as a result of using this book.

All inquiries should be addressed to:
Barron's Educational Series, Inc.
250 Wireless Boulevard
Hauppauge, New York 11788
htt://www.barronseduc.com

Library of Congress Catalog Card No: 2001099774

ISBN 0-7641-5563-6

9 8 7 6 5 4 3 2 1

Separated by United Graphics Pte Ltd
Printed and bound in Singapore by Star Standard Industries (Pte) Ltd

Contents

Introduction

Hi. How are you? Fine and dandy, or moody and miserable? In love with little ol' you or hate the sight of yourself? If you're in the middle of the teen years then you're probably somewhere between the two.

Every woman in the world has been through what you're going through. From supermodels to superstars, they've all been there, and more importantly, made it through to the other side. Physical body changes are one thing; learning how to cope with the new-look you while your emotional self gets a battering is another. But don't panic. This guide will get you through. From your breasts to your butt and everything in between, up and over, you'll be informed and prepared. The world of your body won't be a mystery any longer. And you'll be much happier as a result.

The rules of this book are:

1. There is no perfect body shape

2. There is no perfect weight

3. Everyone is different

4. Everyone looks different

5. Learn to love yourself as yourself.

Got it? Good.

1
head
up

As teens we long to be confident but thanks to Mother Nature, it's not easy. Out of the blue, she kick starts our hormones. All at once, the bodies we've known and loved become mysterious places. We get moody, snappy, and confused. But, don't worry, 'cos every little thing is gonna be alright.

Is This Really Me?

All change! Our bodies start to change around the age of nine, when puberty begins and, it seems, all hell is let loose.

your own personal puberty

EVERYONE GOES THROUGH PUBERTY AT THEIR OWN RATE. No one has the perfect puberty experience—honest. Every one of us will, at some point, look in the mirror and screech, believing we've turned into an alien teen. Not so. You can bet that if your friends were really honest with you, they too have had one breast bigger than the other, odd smells, lumps and bumps, and weird pains where before there was nothing. And every glamour-puss out there has been through just the same.

From being one shape, we start to become another. And it can be oh-so embarrassing. Because it's at that time in our lives when we're not sure if we really want people to notice us very much. Or, if we do, it's got to be on our terms. Whereas once we could wear strappy shirts without thinking twice about it, now the buds of breasts and nipples are suddenly putting in an appearance. This makes most girlies feel very self-conscious—we worry that people are staring at us, at our bodies—and we'd rather run to our room to grab a sweatshirt. About the same time, our legs get hairy, and our armpits aren't much better. Ugh!

The dawn of a new woman

But is it " Ugh" ? Absolutely not. These are all signs that womanhood is just around the corner. And although they throw us off course a little bit, once we know the score, there's nothing to be worried about any more.

you need friends

Yep, this is a time when friends are really important. Not just to have fun with, but to compare notes with. If you feel you're becoming an alien teen thanks to your new body, which you don't recognize, check out how your buddies are looking/feeling. You're all going through similar stuff, so talk and keep talking. Initially you might feel a bit embarrassed but you needn't be. Stand tall and be the first to share how you're really feeling. Your friends will be oh-so grateful.Talking about how your body is changing means no one has to go through this weird time alone. And don't just rely on your buddies. Have an older girlfriend to confide in as well—a Soul Sister—maybe an older cousin, aunt, or trusted family friend. Someone you can open up to and ask questions like "Is it normal to have hairy thighs?"

Puberty Blues

Puberty is when, suddenly, loads of hormones start to be released in great numbers within our bodies.

To begin with we start to get breasts—little buds under our nipples. At about 11, we start to grow taller. The hormones in our bodies make us develop wider hips and narrower waists, and make us look more womanly. Our breasts start to swell. The nipple becomes darker and more prominent, and have you noticed one breast is bigger than the other? This is

hair in new places

When we start finding body hair in new places, we know that puberty is coming. Body hair starts to grow and thicken on our legs, under our arms, and on our genitals. Pubic hair is quite wiry and curly, and it's usually a similar shade to our natural hair color. If you're dark your pubic hair will be dark, if you're fair it will be fair, and so on. But sometimes it can be a completely different color. Just one of Mother Nature's little teasers. Hair growth doesn't happen overnight. Even though it's a gradual change, it can make your body look quite different.

completely normal and will eventually even itself out. But it's worth remembering, as with everything else, that puberty is an individual thing. You could still be flat-chested and bra-less while your best friend is already filling a B-cup bra. All it means is that you are growing at different rates; not even twins experience the same stuff at the same time.

that monthly thing . . .

PERIODS (AKA MENSTRUATION) BEGIN FROM AROUND 12 TO 14, OR SOMETIMES LATER.
Take the time to talk to a mom, aunt, or counselor about periods. Once you have a period it's a sign you are now fertile—able to have a baby. Sooooo, if you're not already informed about birth control, it's time to learn. Because we all know the pregnancy myth that you can't get pregnant the first time you have sex is just that—a myth. You definitely can.

Gina, 18

I was a late bloomer: my body made me look about four years younger than other girls in my grade. It was a miserable time for me. My close friends were cool about it, but others weren't. In gym classes, I'd hide in the corner hoping no one noticed my lack of womanly curves, while other girls pranced around with their breasts and pubic hair. Finally, two days after my 15th birthday, I noticed my breasts were starting to swell. I was soooo excited that I measured myself almost every day! Then, a few months later, I started my period. I was so happy. I felt that at last I belonged. I was a woman.

Growing Pains

There really is such a thing as growing pains, so brace youself 'cos you'll get to know all about them during puberty.

spare yourself the blushes

BLUSHING IS ALL PART OF PUBERTY

Just when we want to be super cool, we end up sputtering and blushing—sounding and looking like a nerd. There's no way around it; sometimes our bodies let us down and leave us feeling very vulnerable when we least need to. Practice being confident in the privacy of your own home. Take a deep breath, hold your head high and speak clearly. As ever, practice makes perfect.

Growing pains are deep aches that are usually felt in the calves, shins, and thighs. Often they seem to come on late at night, and sometimes after we have been very active—but it's not the activity that has caused it.

In fact no one really knows what causes growing pains. It is thought that they are brought on by the sudden surge of growth and change that your body is having to deal with. The best advice for dealing with growing pains is to chill out and not worry about them. If you need some pain relief, ask an adult to give you a heat massage; this will help to relax the muscles. And get some rest. Let your body recharge its batteries.

All out of proportion

Sometimes it can feel like we've grown a foot overnight. Do you ever feel like you're all arms and legs? Yes? Well, guess what? That's normal. Our arms and legs start to grow faster than the rest of us. So for a while we're a bit gangly and dangly, as well as a little clumsier while we get used to our lengthened limbs. If our long arms and legs look a little out of proportion it's only until our torsos catch up.

good news
try to snooze

With all that growing and changing, we need to sleep. It may seem real boring, but without enough of it, our bodies start to struggle. We need deep sleep so all the hormones can do their jobs properly. So remember to get that beauty sleep.

hey up there

How tall we will be when we are adults is usually already decided when we're born. If our Mom and Dad are both six-footers then the chances are we're gonna be tall too. If they're not, then we might stay average height. But often we can inherit our height pattern from our family's gene pool—our grandparents and great-grandparents—and take everyone by surprise. One thing's for sure: keeping to a healthy and normal diet will help us reach our optimal height. We need to eat properly to grow and develop, and a diet without enough natural nutrients can have a bad effect.

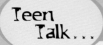

Hair, There, Everywhere

Are you turning into the incredible Yeti woman? No, you're just growing up.

keeping hair at bay

You can shave, pluck, or wax. You can also bleach, not using an ordinary, domestic bleach—that could scar you for life—but a special bleaching cream that's designed for the job.

Where you'll get hair . . .

As we develop into women we start getting hairy. Hair seems to sprout just about everywhere: arms, legs, genital area, top lip, in between your eyebrows, sometimes on your feet, and your toes . . . oh yes, hair really does grow everywhere. Now we don't all get the same hair growth in the same places. Some women have very little body hair, while others are very hairy. Both of these, and everything in between, is normal. If you don't like the hairy parts, you can do something about it.

Getting rid of it

You don't have to if you don't want to. Some European women are cool about leaving their body hair as nature intended, but others prefer to keep their hair at bay. Now this is easily done, but do NOT go for it without a bit of expert

16

instruction. The most popular methods are shaving, tweezing, or waxing—all of which you can do at home. Ask your friendly adult female what she does to keep her body hair in check. Many years of experience will make her a valuable tutor.

when to tackle hair

MOST WOMEN TEND TO WAX OR SHAVE THEIR UNDERARMS AND THEIR LEGS, BUT AVOID DOING IT TOO EARLY
If you have to stand in front of a mirror and peer real close to see the hairs on your legs, then the chances are that you don't need to do a thing just yet. If you have facial hair on your upper lip that is bothering you, get your Mom to take you to a beauty salon where they can bleach it gently.

crimes against eyebrows

The eyebrow is a beautiful thing, which in the hands of a teen with a pair of tweezers can go horribly wrong. No offense, but it's true. They're the kind of things that you don't notice until they look weird. So do not commit a crime against the beauty that is you. Do not pluck your eyebrows to within an inch of their life. Simply remove the hairs that may, or may not, grow in between your brows at the bridge of your nose. And pleeease, leave it at that. Over-plucked eyebrows take a long time to grow back. The natural look, with just a teeny bit of tweaking is best. If you're still not convinced, take a close look at how female celebrities treat their eyebrows with respect.

17

Skinplicity

You spend your whole life living inside your skin; here's a quick guide to the do's and don'ts of looking after your skin.

growing makes its mark on you

Because we tend to grow in such rapid bursts when we're teens, we can end up with marks where our skin has suddenly had to stretch. These are the much-dreaded stretchmarks. Though some girls get them, most young girls don't. They usually turn up on our thighs, butt, stomach, and breasts. There is NO cream that will get rid of them, but in time, they will change from the angry red lines into faint silvery ones that you barely notice. If you're really bothered by them, slap on some fake tan. Problem solved!

Know your skin type

Is your skin type normal, sensitive, oily, dry, or combination? Don't know? Then read on:

● Does your skin flare up, and get red or flushed easily? Then you probably have sensitive skin. Always use gentle products with "hypoallergenic" on the label. Never use harsh cleansers.

● Do you feel your makeup slides off your skin? If so, you probably have oily skin. So always choose non-greasy products, and cleanse regularly.

● Do you seem to have shiny skin along your forehead and nose? Then you probably have combination skin, with oily skin on the area known as the T-zone 'cos it's a "T" shape.

Hey, clever stuff! So, use a cleanser and concealer if you need to on the T-zone and then choose gentler, hypoallergenic products for use everywhere else.

● Some girls are lucky enough to have skin without any specific type, known as " normal" (don't you just hate that word?) skin. You girls need to maintain your healthy glow and don't gunk your face with too many products/makeup.

If you've never had a daily cleansing routine, now is the time to reconsider as puberty takes hold. Without your help, it can take up to 25 days for your skin to rid itself of dirt and stale makeup. You don't want that hanging around, do you?

cellulite

Cellulite is where you get dimply skin, often on your thighs and butt. It's not pleasant, but it's a bit like getting your period—part of being a woman. There is no cure for it, but it's hardly life threatening so don't worry about it. There are expensive creams and treatments that claim to zap it, but none of them work long term. If you get cellulite, so what? It affects thin people, fat people, medium-weight people; we're all in the same boat on this one. Besides, unless you're very heavy in your teens, it isn't something you're likely to have to worry about until you're older.

19

Hey, Zitface

Just when we need to look and feel better than ever, Mother Nature sends in the zits to wreak havoc and make our lives hell.

when do zits become acne?

ALL ZITS ARE CALLED ACNE, WHETHER YOU'VE GOT THREE OR THREE THOUSAND

If you have a large number of red, angry zits, ie. more than just your average teenage zits, get them diagnosed by your healthcare provider or a dermatologist. They can prescribe steroid creams which might, or might not, help. Often, a specific type of oral contraceptive can help clear acne. Discuss it and see what they feel is best for you. And, remember, those zits will go.

The reality is that zits and acne are part and parcel of teendom. Sorry about the bad news but there's no getting away from it. At times, puberty has the swiftness of lightning: we might go to bed wearing our baby soft, smooth, and blemish-free skin with pride, then at the stroke of midnight puberty strikes, and we wake up next morning as ZitGirl.

Yes, we have the technology to eradicate them, but patience is required. There are no miracle creams, special spot sticks, or zappers that will banish them overnight, so don't be bamboozled into spending a fortune on stuff. Nothing will cure your zits; they'll go, eventually, once your hormones settle down. And not before.

Tackling the enemy

Washing and cleansing the zit-zone will help. Use warm water, cotton balls, gentle soap, tea-tree cream, or any water-based cleansers. Resist harsh cleansers though, as alcohol- and hexachlorophene-based products can make your skin really dry and flaky and may cause irritation. And stop squeezing and zapping! You may scar yourself and spread the bacteria that caused the zit in the first place.

hiding those zitty critters

When you've got a hot date, hide those unwanted zits with a mild, concealer stick—some medicated ones can be harsh. And go steady with the face cake or you'll look worse instead of better.

why do we get zits?

During puberty, glands in our skin get over-stimulated by hormones and produce too much of their oily secretions. These clog our skin pores, then bacteria form, and zits are the way our skin reacts to these bacteria. Complicated eh? Emotional stress, being run-down or over-tired can be a trigger too. So keep chilled, relax, and get some decent sleep.

Usually we get zits on our face, but they can also crop up on our back, chest, and neck. Research has yet to show a link between diet and zits, but to give our skin the nourishment it needs, we should aim to eat at least five portions of mixed fruit and vegetables a day.

21

Treat Yourself

If you really must squeeze zits, always follow this routine but remember never to squeeze a red, angry spot. It's not ready. You'll end up pushing the bacteria further into your skin. The result? An angrier, redder zit. If it has a yellow head, or is a black-head, it's ready for zapping.

gonna zap that zit out of my life

- Always be careful around the delicate eye area. Avoid scrubbing away with your normal cleanser; use a special eye makeup removing product.
- Boost your skin's appearance—gently massage your daily moisturizer with feather-light fingers all over your face, then remove with warm, damp, cotton ball.
- If you are trying out a spot-zapper product, give it two months. If it hasn't made a difference by then, it never will.
- Choose products labeled non-comedongenic. These still allow the skin to function normally, and so prevent clogged pores, which can only be a good thing.
- Drink plenty of water. Your body—and your skin—always need the moisture.

You will need:
- A towel
- Cotton pads
- Mirror

Fill a basin with very hot water—not boiling—and be careful. Hold your head over the water with a towel over your head so the steam from the water and rising heat can hit your face and help your pores open up. Wash your hands. Then, with a cotton pad on each finger, very gently squeeze either side of the offending zits. Don't use your nails or you'll damage your skin. Wipe the gunk away with cotton, then splash with cool water to help your pores close up again. Wash your hands. Job done, minimum cost, minimum fuss. Afterward, use a very mild cleanser, followed by a light moisturizer.

zits zits stay away

For a zit-free zone:
Keep your face fresh
Don't sleep in makeup.
Don't use harsh products
too frequently
Drink plenty of water
Eat fruit and fresh vegetables

give your face a feast

The day before: Take half a pint of witch hazel, two tablespoons of dried rose petals, and two sprigs of rosemary. Put these in an airtight container and give them a real good shake. Leave in the fridge overnight, then strain into another container. The liquid is your very own brand of rose-petal toner.
Then make up a face pack: Thoroughly mix a sensitive-skin light moisturizer with a couple of spoonfuls each of honey and oats. Leave in the fridge to cool along with thinly sliced circles of cucumber. Apply the mask liberally to face and neck, and place a slice of cucumber over each eye. Chill out, listening to your fave vibes. Wash off and use your own rose-petal toner to finish. Blisstastic or what?

23

Hair Care

Our hair is the one way we can change the way we look, without changing who we are.

We all love it when our hair has that just-washed, shiny, soft, lovely feel to it. So how do we make sure our hair stays strong and healthy? It couldn't be easier—just wash and go.

the simple rule for fab hair

TO KEEP YOUR HAIR HEALTHY, WASH AND CONDITION IT REGULARLY.
Don't believe everything cosmetic manufacturers try to sell us. If you use too many products, you'll end up with a buildup that can make your hair look dull and lifeless.

As with everything else, different people have different hair types: black, afro, blonde, ginger, auburn, mousy. The thing with your hair is, if you hate it—change it. Hair is the one thing we can experiment with without causing any lasting damage.

Bad hair day

A bad hairdo can feel like the end of the world. So, if you fancy a spiky, short, urchin crop instead of your flowing locks, think it through first. Your hair will grow back, but it takes time. Most of us have had our hair cut and thought, "Whhhyyyy did I do that!" So if you want a radical new style, find a salon that can generate a computer image of how you might look with your new style. Just don't get something that you know you'll never be able to re-create at home.

finish off with a little gloss

Even the shiniest of hair needs a helping hand, so, for that extra finish, try using a light gloss product to give you that extra boost.

hair today, gone tomorrow

What would happen if your hair fell out? Well, like two million other U.S. teens you would cope, but it wouldn't be easy. Alopecia, a condition that results in hair loss, isn't common in teens, but it can happen. For some it's only ever a small patch of hair, while others lose all their head hair, or even their body hair. If you are experiencing some hair loss, don't panic. Yes, your hair is part of you, but it's not all of who you are. Let off steam to let people know how you're feeling. But the best thing to do is talk; log on to www.alopeciakids.com to find out how other teens cope.

Trichotillomania, or compulsive hair-pulling, is a psychological disorder that can cause baldness. Kids and teens repeatedly pull their hair out, often making their scalp bleed and creating bald patches. It might start as a little habit, but you need to get help before it becomes a big problem. Contact your local healthcare provider or call the Trichotillomania Learning Center at 831-457-1004.

2

treasure
your
chest

Some of us can't wait to get breasts, 'cos they make us feel really womanly and sexy. For others, breasts are a constant source of worry. Are they big enough? Too big? Odd sizes? Odd shape? Are the nipples too big? Too small? Too dark? The list is endless. Forget it. "Perfect" breast shape does not exist.

Breasts Glorious Breasts

When our bodies start to grow and become more womanly, we are changing like a caterpillar into a butterfly. Ahhh . . .

can our nipples get erect?

YES, THEY REALLY DO GET ERECT. And guess what? It's completely normal. Our nipples can get hard and stick out when we're cold, nervous, or sexually excited. They are very responsive to touch, so much so that just friction from your bra or top can cause them to stick out. If you get embarrassed by this, which is understandable, just put on a sweater or fold your arms across your chest.

Breasts: whether we love 'em or hate 'em, we've got them for life. So it's a good idea to learn to love them. Our breasts start to grow around the age of 10 to 14. That's only a guide. It can happen earlier or later. If you've already started your periods, but your breasts are still just buds, maybe it's worth going to see your doctor. But remember that we all grow at different rates.

The aureola is the darker area of skin on our breasts, aka nipples. They can be anything from pale pink to almost black, big or small, protruding or inverted. Whatever they are, don't get flustered—they are yours, just as they were meant to be.

Inverted nipples are when, instead of having a protruding nipple, they are like little slits, almost turned in on themselves. Sometimes they pop out, sometimes they don't, but you can still get sexual pleasure from them, and you can still breast-feed, which is the nipple's main biological function. If you get a clear, milky white fluid from your nipples, don't worry; it's the way our body keeps the nipple ducts open and flushed through. BUT if this discharge is more like pus, or has blood in it, go to your family healthcare provider, because it could indicate that something is wrong.

breast hair
beware

Puberty sometimes give us hair on our breasts and nipples. If you don't like the hairs, gently tweeze them out. But take care, as tweezing can sometimes result in a red zit or mark.

keeping a
balanced view

JUST LIKE OUR FEET—WHERE ONE IS USUALLY HALF A SIZE SMALLER THAN THE OTHER—OUR BREASTS CAN DIFFER SLIGHTLY IN SIZE TOO. Normally you're the only person to notice this because you have a bird's-eye view, looking down on them. So try to be calm and rational about it. From the front, can anyone else really tell, without staring at your chest and having it pointed out to them? If you feel it is very noticeable, then you can always get a pad to fill out the other side a bit. Some girls find that even after they have finished growing, one breast is a full cup size bigger than the other.

29

Basic Maintenance

As the proud new owner of breasts, you'll want to learn how to keep them healthy.

Your breasts are a key feature of your new womanly shape and often the focus of sexual attention. They should make you feel good about yourself, but you must take care of them too. Look after them now and they'll stay fine for as long as you do. Stretchmarks can crop up on your breasts, especially when you have a growth spurt. This is normal, and although you can't do anything to zap them away, they will fade in time.

lumps and bumps

It's a good idea to start self-examination early so you get to know what is normal for your breasts. Check yourself in the middle of your menstrual cycle each month. Most breast lumps turn out to be completely harmless. If you find a lump in one breast, check the other one; if you have a corresponding lump there, it's probably normal for you. If your mom or sister has had breast cancer, you have a higher risk of developing it yourself. And if you find a lump, visit your family healthcare provider. It's most likely not to be cancer, but if it is, the sooner it is treated, the better.

Painful breasts?

This could be caused by a growing spurt—and should be brief—or it could be due to the hormones released when you have your period. Known as cyclical mastalgia, the pain should only last a day or so. Breast pain can also be caused by a cyst in the breast tissue. This is a harmless, fluid-filled lump that is easily treated. If you are worried, visit your family healthcare provider.

monthly ups, and downs

Some girls go up a full cup size during their period, while others just experience a lot of tenderness. To reduce the soreness of swollen breasts, try wearing a cotton bra that gives plenty of support.

How to self-examine

One of the easiest times to do this is while you shower. Raise your arm and reach behind your head with one hand. Using the palm of your other hand, gently feel around the outside of your breast and into your armpit. Do this on both sides. When you leave the shower, dry yourself and then look at your breasts. See what their normal shape is; lift your arm up on each side too. Any puckering of the skin, dimpling, nipple discharge or sudden nipple inversion should be checked out by your local healthcare provider.

Bra·vo

You might prefer undershirts, but you don't want saggy breasts, do you? Well, wear the right support and you won't get them.

It's a medical fact that once breasts sag or stretch, they don't spring back. This is because the ligament that gives our breasts their uplift stretches with weight gain or lack of support, and it can't go back to its original length. Therefore, we get droopy breasts—it's known in the medical world as Cooper's Droop. Weird but true.

These days there are hundreds of great bras, so you've absolutely no excuse for not wearing one. If you don't want to draw attention to your bust, get a nice plain T-shirt bra,

cracking the code for bra sizes

You probably know the measurement lingo by heart—such as 32B, 36C—but what does it all mean? It's a bit like a secret code, but it's very easy to crack. Ready? Let's go. The numbers relate to the width of your back, the letters to the cup or breast size. How simple is that? To find your cup size, measure around your body directly under your breasts, then measure the fullest part of your chest. The difference between these two measurements gives you the cup size. If the difference is 0, you're an A cup; 1 in. is a B cup; 2 in. is a C cup; 3 in. is a D cup; 4 in. is a DD cup, and so on.

or, if you love all things lacy and girlie, go for ultra glam. But whichever one you choose, it has to fit properly. Get your breasts measured and bra fit checked every six months. As we develop, our breasts can grow or change shape slightly. Our breasts usually reach their full size by the time we're 17 or 18, but changes in our weight and hormone levels can cause them to keep on changing. So keep a check on your breasts. They'll love you for it!

bra hitches

Problem: Your breasts bulge at the top or sides of your bra.
Answer: Cup size is too small. Golden rule—your breast should be encased in the cup.

Problem: Your bra rides up your back.
Answer: The back strap is too big. Try a size smaller, such as going from a 36 to a 34.

Problem: You're left with shoulder strap marks.
Answer: The back of your bra is probably too big, or you are wearing the shoulder straps too tight. The support for your bra should come from the back strap, not your shoulder straps.

Plus if you wear an under-wire bra, the wires should sit flat; if they poke outward, then the cup size is too small.

Getting to Know You

Because our parts are all tucked up inside us, there's an air of mystery about them.

Just like the names that kids make up when they don't know the right word for something, there are a whole lotta names for the vagina. They're usually used by guys, 'cos they don't really know much about it. So let's be mature young ladies and call the vagina a vagina, because we're just about to get acquainted with ours.

say whaaaaaat?

Weird words aren't they? Here's how to say 'em.
vagina: say ver-gina
vulva: say vul-va
labia: say la-bee-a
clitoris: say clit-orr-is

Vaginas—what you need to know

Our vagina is actually the part of us which is inside. It's the channel through which we give birth, have our period, and it's where a guy's penis enters when we have penetrative sex. The bits we can see have a host of different names. And to talk you through it, why not get a mirror and let's do our own vaginal exam. By now you probably have some pubic hair, and in the middle you have an opening, which is the entrance to the vagina. The tissues outside your vagina are known as

34

the vulva. Either side of your vaginal opening you have some outer lips which are called the outer labia. Working inwards, you then have inner labia (inner lips). Towards the front of your vulva is the clitoris, which is designed for pure pleasure.

the clitoris and the G-spot

The clitoris is incredibly sensitive—just like the tip of a guy's penis—and has no other function than to give us pleasure when it is stimulated. Three cheers for the clitoris! The G-spot is another part of our vagina that can be sexually stimulated. It's up on the upper side of the vagina, deep inside us.

to boldly go

"I really didn't like what I saw the first time I examined myself. It all looked so raw and crude—I couldn't imagine ever letting a guy get to know that part of my body! The next time I knew what to expect, and started to feel more comfortable with my body. (Sylvie, 15)

"What really surprised me was just how ticklish some parts of me felt, as I explored inside my body. I had no idea that the inner lips were so sensitive to touch." (Laura, 16)

"It wasn't until my first serious relationship that I realized I didn't really know a whole lot about my body. Armed with a mirror, I shut myself away in a bedroom one evening and discovered a whole new side to me." (Shireen, 18)

Vagina Care

Just because vaginas are hidden away,
doesn't mean they should be left out of
your hygiene routine

Part of growing into being a woman is that you will have some
vaginal discharge. This discharge doesn't make you dirty. OK?

how to wash your vagina

Use warm water, and if you
want, a mild, gentle soap to
gently, note the word gently,
wash your vulva. Highly
perfumed soaps/bath bubbles
or gels can cause irritation.

Vaginal discharge is absolutely normal
and tends to be the gunk we don't need
(vaginas are self-cleaning). It's usually a
creamy or whitish color and it will probably change throughout our monthly
cycle. Any different discharge is the first
sign of possible infection. For instance
thrush, a yeast infection, can be caused by upsetting the normal yeast balance within the vagina. This sometimes happen
if we douche (see the box opposite), have taken antibiotics (a
common cause of yeast infection), or it might be a sensitivity
reaction to condoms, or even washing powders.

Any kind of discharge that you don't think is normal
needs to be checked by your gynecologist. Don't be embarrassed; ask to be seen by a female and if you need to, take

a friend for support. If your discharge bothers you, just because it's there, then for extra confidence you can wear a panty liner. If this helps you, then do it.

what's that smell?

Our vulvas do have a smell, but if you are healthy and so is your vulva, it's not unpleasant. If you start to get a fishy/yeasty odor, that is a sign you could have an infection. For treatment you should see your gynecologist. Don't leave it, it'll only get worse.

to douche or not to douche

What is a douche? A douche is a wash that women are supposed to use to freshen up their vaginas. But hold on, who says our vagina smells bad? The truth is that it doesn't. We do have a smell down there but it's not something other people can detect; it's too subtle. And our vaginas are self-cleaning. Using a commercial product to douche might do more harm than good. Why, you ask? Well, our vaginas are home to good bacteria as well as bad. Daily gentle washing, bathing or showering gets rid of the bad stuff, but douching gets rid of the good stuff too. This can leave us more prone to infections. So, leave well alone. Douches are for dunces. And that's not us.

Vaginal Exams

Oooh. Not pleasant whatever you way you think of them, but they're a necessary part of being a woman today.

what does a pap smear tell us?

Pap smears are very important for your health. Once you are sexually active, you must have regular tests. They test for abnormal cell changes, which can be an indicator of a risk of cancer. If abnormal cells are found they are easily treated. You can, always ask to be seen by a female practitioner. Take a friend/family member with you for support if you want to.

If you are thinking about becoming sexually active, then now is the time to have your first vaginal exam. Because all our bits are inside us we sometimes need internal exams to be sure we are healthy down there. These can be uncomfortable, but aren't really painful. For a step-by-step guide of what happens at an exam, log on to www.firstvisit.org. Meanwhile, here's a quick guide and remember the doctor has seen it all before, a zillion times, so don't worry about what he/she might think.

What happens

You'll have to lie on your back for the exam. A bedsheet will be placed over the lower half of your body and you'll need to put your feet into stirrups, bring your knees up and let them flop to the side. To be able to get to your cervix, the doctor needs to insert a conical instrument called a speculum, which pushes aside the

just clear your throat

During the exam, give a little cough just before they put the speculum in; this will help to relax your vaginal muscles.

vaginal walls so he can take cell scrapings from your cervix. Sometimes he will put a warm gel around the entrance to your vagina, which may be uncomfortable, but should rarely hurt. If it does, let the doctor know; maybe you need slightly gentler handling. Sometimes after a pap smear you might get a little bit of spotting. Take a panty liner with you just in case.

julie-ann, 19

I got in such a state about my first pap smear, but everyone—the doctor, the nurse, the receptionist—did their best to help me relax. What helped me most was the doctor simply talking me through the whole procedure before he started. Of course, it felt strange lying on a couch with no panties on and my knees in the air but I knew it was important to have the test and that I would feel reassured to know everything was in working order. Yes, it's a bit of a shock when the speculum is inserted, but only because it feels so cold.

3

periods:
the
lowdown

Menstruation happens to all women. The age we start our monthly bleed varies according to our genes, but whenever it happens, it is a cause to be happy. It means we are becoming a woman. There's no need to shout it from the rooftops; but we shouldn't be embarrassed either. And there's no need to worry about it. Period.

Millstone or Milestone?

Part of becoming a woman, in the physical sense at least, is getting your period.

Our bodies are quite wonderful things in the way that they work. Understanding how they work is the best way of getting to know them. Here's a bit of biology to explain why periods happen. It's not at all technical, so pleeeeease read on. Every month we produce hormones that stimulate our egg factories—ovaries—and our bodies to prepare for having a

warning: period due

"A couple of days before my period, this huge red zit erupts on my chin—it never fails. It used to get me down, but now I just treat it as an excuse to spend an evening soaking in the bath and pampering myself." (Evie, 16)

"It was my friends who first noticed how tense and irritable I became just days before my period. I tend to get really wound up and lash out at people for the slightest reason. Now that I'm aware of it, I try to steer clear of situations that are likely to set me off. I find that I don't sleep very well either before my period arrives, but going for a swim or a jog seems to help chill me out." (Beth, 18)

baby. The womb gets ready for a fertilized egg to implant itself. When this doesn't happen our bodies get rid of the thickened womb lining, which comes away as a bloody flow through our vagina. Then, the body starts the whole cycle again. For most of us,

estrogen and progesterone

Estrogen is esential for normal sexual development and maintenance of the reproductive system, which is your womb, ovaries, and fallopian tubes. Progesterone is also a must-have to keep all of these working properly. When you ovulate—release an egg—your body makes more progesterone, which causes the lining of the womb to thicken ready to accept a fertilized egg.

our periods run in a cycle of about 28 days, but it can be longer or shorter than this. As with everything else, each of us is different.

Hormones—who needs 'em?

Estrogen and progesterone are the two hormones—chemical messengers—that trigger all the weird girlie stuff. Too much or too little of them can cause blips, such as mood swings, increased zits, and painful periods. All fairly normal in a girl's development. But if you feel you are suffering too much at the hands of these two culprits, go to see your healthcare provider who should be able to help.

What is a Period?

It's the time when, once a month, you bleed for about four to five days.

Also known as menstruation, a period has lots of nicknames, such as the "curse" or "being on the rag," but they all refer to the same thing. Lots of girlies get freaked out by them, worry what it's all about, and get quite confused. The facts are:

- periods are normal
- they are healthy
- they don't mean you're dirty

Tasha, 17

Lucky for me I was at school when I had my first period. I was terrified I would have these awful cramps, and gush blood everywhere for everyone to see. But it wasn't like that, thank goodness. I had a bit of diarrhea the night before and the next day at school, just after lunch, I had an urge to go to the bathroom. I urinated, then wiped myself and there was some blood on the tissue. That was it—no great gushing moment. I didn't have a pad with me, nor did I want to go asking my friends for one, so I went to the school nurse. She was really helpful and gave me a couple to last till I got home.

Period blood is simply the thickened lining of your womb and just looks like blood. But it can look very different from what you imagine. Sometimes it's a brownish discharge, other times it's bright red, and at other times it's so dark it looks black. All of which are quite normal. But if you are ever worried, don't keep it to yourself: you must go to your gynecologist.

what to expect on the first time

Your first period is unlikely to be a gushing flow of blood. Usually you get a headache, some cramping, and a few spots of blood. If you're worried you might get caught out then keep a sanitary pad in your bag. Having something with you will take away that anxiety.

Jilli, 16

One morning I woke up and found blood spots on my bed sheets; I was *sooo* embarrassed that I whipped them off the bed as quickly as possible so that I could hide the evidence. But I was too late. My mom walked in just as I was trying to stuff the sheet into the laundry basket. I needn't have worried though 'cos she was so cool about it all. She ran me a bubble bath, let me stay home from school, and gave me a goody bag of sanitary pads and tampons. It hasn't been easy as my periods are always very painful, but my mom went through exactly the same stuff, so she knows how I feel.

Easing the Pain

Unfortunately for some of us, our periods will bring some physical discomfort.

There's no need to suffer period pains in silence, so don't let them dominate your life. Over-the-counter prescriptions from the drugstore can ease menstrual cramps and headaches. Always follow the instructions on the packet and never take more than the stated dose. If standard painkillers don't help, try herbal remedies or visit your gynecologist for advice. WARNING: If you have a heavy period with clotting, extreme pain, diarrhea, or vomiting, you must make sure to see your gynecologist promptly.

try these when it really hurts

FOR ABDOMINAL CRAMPS TRY:
- A warm bath
- A hot water bottle on your tummy
- Having someone massage your lower back
- Going for a walk to take your mind off it
- Some gentle exercise; when we exercise our bodies produce naturally occurring pain-killers, such as endorphins and serotonin, in our system

Better diet—better mood?

Because of the hormones going crazy in our bodies before a period we can get moody, snappy, or irritable. The medical name for this is premenstrual syndrome (PMS). Not everyone experiences this, but if you do, look for ways of keeping more balanced during the PMS blues. Try evening primrose oil tablets; they take a few months to work. Also make sure your diet includes plenty of fresh fruit and vegetables. Some studies have linked PMS with a lack of dietary magnesium and vitamin B6, which can all be found in those lovely fruit and veggies. If you find your PMS is taking charge of your life, you know what to do—go see your gynecologist.

two women one cycle

Sometimes women who live together end up having their periods at the same time. It's called menstrual synchrony and no one really understands why it happens.

if your periods stop

If you have been having regular periods and they stop, there is a reason why. Have you been dieting? If so, getting too thin can prevent your periods. This is very unhealthy. You must seek out help. Call in at your local women's health center. Have you had unprotected sex? You know what I'm gonna say. Yep, you could be pregnant. Get a home pregnancy testing kit or call your family healthcare provider. For confidential help and advice call the Planned Parenthood Federation of America on 1-800-230-PLAN (24-hour hotline).

Absorbing Stuff

Here's a guide to sanitary protection. One thing's for sure, it's way better than the stuff our moms had to use a few years ago.

If you're new to sanitary protection, then here's a guide to what there is and how to use it. Even if you know all you need to about sanitary protection, check out the next few pages to see if there's a handy tip or two that you could use.

Sanitary napkins

These pads sit in the gusset of your underpants and are placed right up against your crotch area to absorb any blood that comes from your vagina. If you're new to periods, then you're better off using a sanitary napkin. They're easier to use and a little less scary than inserting a tampon. (More on that later.) These days sanitary napkins are very effective at absorbing your flow. You can get all kinds and shapes and sizes and you really have to try out different brands to see which ones suit you best. And you can get them pretty much anywhere. If you're embarrassed about buying them, ask your mom to pick some up for you. Sanitary napkins and used tampons cannot be flushed down the toilet, and even if they could, they would end up in our oceans. So, be environmentally cool too and get rid of them in your garbage.

pad tips

- Always go for a pad with a sticky base, so that it stays put
- Pads with sticky side tabs as well as a sticky base give you even more confidence that your pad is staying in position
- The amount of blood you lose will vary during your period—again each woman is slightly different—so you might need different types of protection throughout the month. Maybe start off with a thick pad for more absorbency and work down to a thinner one toward the end of the flow.
- Change your pad regularly. This helps you keep hygienic and also makes sure you avoid any spillage! Changing your pad every three to four hours during the day is about right.
- Sometimes, if you have a very heavy flow, you might need to wear a tampon and a pad. Again, this is normal.
- Of course you can't wake/don't want to wake in the night to change your pad. Don't worry: you can buy special nighttime pads, which are more absorbent than regular pads.

All About Tampons

Worn inside the body, tampons let you exercise freely or wear tight pants!

routine practice for tampon safety

- Always use the tampon with the smallest absorbency so that you don't leave it in for too long
- Change your tampon every three to four hours
- During your period use a sanitary napkin to give your body a break from tampons. Try using sanitary napkins at night and at other times when you are unable to change tampons frequently.
- Practice good hygiene: wash your hands thoroughly before and after inserting a tampon
- Always read the manufacturer's leaflet, which has regularly updated information about TSS

Tampons are cylinder-shaped bits of cotton wadding with a slightly rounded tip at one end and some string at the other. You insert these into your vagina where they absorb any blood from your period. They come in two types: ones with a soft cardboard applicator and ones without. And there are about four different levels of absorbency to cope with light through to heavy flows of blood. As you start your period you'll probably just need the lightest flow tampon, but you'll be able to judge this better, as you get used to having your periods.

The first few times you use a tampon it's bound to feel a little strange. But not uncomfortable, as your vagina is almost designed to accept something like this. The vaginal muscles clamp it in place. But it **shouldn't** hurt and it **shouldn't** fall out. If it does either of these, it's in the wrong place. Take it out and start again. The worst you can do is to stress about it: if you get worked up, your body will be tense, making it even more difficult to insert a tampon.

tampons and virginity

Sometimes people wrongly suggest if you have used a tampon you aren't a virgin. This is completely untrue. You are a virgin until you have penetrative sex.

toxic shock syndrome

You must change your tampon every few hours—regardless of whether it has reach full absorbency or not. This helps maintain vaginal health and protects against the possible risk of Toxic Shock Syndrome (TSS). This is a very rare, but potentially life-threatening condition, caused by a poison produced by bacteria. The link between tampon use and TSS remains unclear but case studies suggest that young women using tampons and absorbency levels are key factors. Several signs and symptoms can accompany TSS, including diarrhea, fainting, a high fever, muscle pain, and a sunburn-like rash. If you suspect you might have TSS symptoms, remove the tampon right away—this stops bacterial growth in 80 percent of cases—and go to see your local healthcare provider as soon as possible.

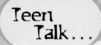

Using a Tampon

OK. This might seem like a nightmare job.
But it's not. Practice, in this case,
certainly does make perfect.

If you can't feel comfortable with your body then, you're
going to lose this battle. When using a tampon you need to
get it in position up in your vagina. To do this, either use the
applicator supplied, which means
your finger doesn't have to go
too far inside, or just use a finger.
You might want to insert your finger first so you can get an idea
of just what you are trying to do
and where you're aiming to posi-
tion the tampon. Now the best way to do this is to have a little privacy—of course. In your bathroom, stand with one leg
resting on something—say the toilet rim. This just gives you
easier access! Take the tampon out of its wrapping and
make sure that the string is hanging downward away from
the tampon. Give it a gentle tug to make sure it's firmly
attached to the tampon. Now carefully put the tampon in,

going with the flow

As you get to know your
menstrual cycle, you will find
which absorbency best suits
your light and heavy days: mini
tampons are for light flows
and super or superplus are
for heavy flows.

52

rounded tip first, aiming up and slightly toward the base of your spine. If using an applicator, push gently and the tampon will be pushed out into position. Then you withdraw the applicator—and the tampon stays in place. If using your finger, you push it up a couple of inches—but not too far.

when using a tampon

DO wash your hands before and after insertion

DO change them every few hours or more often if your flow is heavy

DO put a fresh tampon in before going to bed and when you wake in the morning

NEVER put more than one tampon inside you at a time

NEVER reuse a tampon

rescuing a lost tampon

It does happen. What you need to do is go back to stage 1 when you inserted it. Go to the bathroom, stand with one leg raised and carefully and gently feel inside you for the string. The cervix at the very end of the vagina inside you is closed to the size of a pinhead, so nothing can get beyond it. If you can't find it, you must get someone else to get it out, otherwise you will be at risk of infection. Ask your mom or soul sister to help. If you can't, or she won't, ask your best friend. If she won't you must go to your doctor or local ER. You might feel embarrassed, but there's no need. They've seen it all before.

All Part of the Package

And what about those optional extras that your period brings with it?

don't be paranoid

Your sensitivity is heightened when you have your period, which is why you think everyone is staring at you!

Puberty also brings with it, headaches, extra zits, greasy hair, and mood swings. All because our bodies suddenly have loads more hormones buzzing around inside them creating havoc. All of these things can throw us into despair, but are completely normal and easy to solve. And, best of all, they don't last that long.

how to avoid the embarrassment

If you start unexpectedly and don't have a sanitary pad at hand, wrap a load of tissue paper around the crotch of your panties. This makeshift pad will absorb the flow until you can get proper sanitary wear. And while menstruating, avoid clothing that is too tight and steer clear of pale colors on your lower half, just in case you have a leak.

Oh no, it's B.O.

Once we hit puberty we start to smell a bit different. We tend to sweat more once our hormones have kicked in, and we can sweat in all kinds of places: our hands, our feet, under our arms, in between our thighs, behind our knees, in between the cheeks of our rear end, places we didn't even know existed! Sweating is fine. It's normal. It's how your body cools down. Sometimes sweat has a smell to it, but that's easily washed away. The only way we actually get body odor (B.O.) is by wearing clothes that have dried sweat on them, or by not keeping ourselves clean. Don't go getting paranoid. A daily wash with mild soap is all you need to keep whiffiness at bay.

make all the fuss you want

PAMPER YOURSELF DURING YOUR PERIOD

Wash your hair, have long, warm baths—hot water can ease your cramps too. And if you feel run-down, lie on your bed with some cucumber slices on your eyes and listen to your favorite music.

bikini zone

To shave or not to shave? Shaving your pubic area is a personal choice. Some girls just do their bikini line; others want the whole thing off. Whether it's the natural look, shaving or waxing the bikini zone, or going naked down there, the choice should always be up to you. Don't let others pressure you into doing something else. It's your body, therefore your decision. One tip though: if you want to shave it all off—which is not recommended—you can cut yourself or get razor burn. You are also at risk of in-grown hairs, which can get infected and will itch real bad when they come back in. So don't dare to be bare—it ain't worth it!

4

together forever

OK. You've got your brand new bod, so stand proud. The skin you're in has to last your whole adult life, so love it. The rules are that you do not disrespect your body. Be cool, be confident, and accept that your look is THE look. Don't let yourself be influenced by distorted body images. Love yourself, always.

Body Confidence

This is the part which you have to read,
reread, and read again. Why? 'Cos it tells
you the absolute truth about bodies and how
to stay cool about the whole thing.

three little facts
to learn by heart

FACT 1
Beauty is in the eye
of the beholder

FACT 2
Being thin is not the key
to being beautiful

FACT 3
No one has the perfect body

OK. Us teens can get obsessed with image. We want to fit in, look hot, and strut our stuff. Know what? It can all be done without stressing over size and looks. We are all individuals, which means there is no perfect body shape and no perfect size. Our society is obsessed with women being thin, having flat tummies, pert breasts, and cute butts. As informed teen queens, we want to be healthy, active, and to show society that real women look and love to be different.

Stars in their eyes

Noticed how "stars" always look like complete babes in their pictures? Well they don't just fall out of bed looking like that.

Their "beauty" is an image, created with makeup, salon haircare, and expensive clothes. Check out their poses: they all have their favorite stance. The one that shows them in their best light—and hides their least favorite body parts. Behind the gloss, they all have their bad hair days, bad skin days, and fat days. We just don't get to see them.

pump up your pride

THERE'S NO QUICK FIX TO BUILD YOUR BODY CONFIDENCE, BUT YOU CAN HELP YOURSELF FEEL BETTER ABOUT THE VERY LUVVERLY YOU:

- Don't compare yourself to the hyped-up stars. You're you, with your own qualities and charms.
- Don't diss yourself, your body, or your looks. Be happy and true to yourself. Don't let other people's looks, opinions, or ideals make you feel you are any less worthy as a person in your own right.

are you body confident?

Take our quick test to find out.
- When someone grabs the camera or camcorder, do you run for cover?
- Do you prefer loose baggy clothing?
- Do you always think other people would look better than you do in your clothes?
- Do you hate going swimming?
- When trying on clothes will you always use a sealed-off cubicle?
- When you walk down the street, do you hunch over, keeping your eyes to the ground?

If you answered "Yes" to any three of these then the chances are that your body confidence needs a booster . . . and fast!

Listen Up, Sisters

Think you're the only one with a body
that's the wrong shape? You've got company.

Karen, 20

I loved dancing: tap, modern, ballet, but I
hated the leotard and leggings. Everyone could
stare at the pot belly I had inherited from my
mother; she was exactly the same body shape—
tall with a pot belly. It was embarrassing the
way that my tummy protruded from beneath every
waistband. Boys taunted me and girls laughed
whenever I danced in those dreaded leotards.
Even my dance teacher instructed me to lose
some pounds. ". . . and start doing sit-ups,"
she ordered, "at least 50 a day. You need to
get rid of that fat tummy." I tried dieting,
but it only made it look bigger, because I lost
weight from everywhere but my stomach.

One day, I decided to try on my mother's
stomach-flattening girdle and it worked. After
that, I saved up to buy my own control pants.
It was ridiculous, a teenager wearing a girdle,
but it made me feel more confident. Of course,
I couldn't wear it all the time—gym lessons and
dates were all very dangerous in case anyone
glimpsed my secret, but when I wanted to feel
thinner I would pull the girdle on and feel a

size smaller. It was three years before I realized my Rubens-like tummy was feminine. I actually look upon it now as sexy and womanly. If only I'd known that as a teenager.

Being stick thin with a washboard stomach is not the norm. Sure you can do sit-ups, watch what you eat and dress sensibly (no crop tops or hipster jeans for those with rounded bellies) but nothing will ultimately change your body shape. It's easier—and makes you happier—to accept yourself as you are.

Emma, 17

While I was at high school I was always really skinny—it was just my natural body shape, but boy was I made to feel bad about it. All my friends, who were just normal girls, not fat, not thin, normal, almost pushed me out of the group as soon as they started talking about clothes and size. They would moan about having fat thighs or a sticky-out tummy while all I wanted was some more weight on my legs and arms. But as soon as I opened my mouth, they turned on the ice-cold glares. How dare I think of joining in the conversation? I was thin! They almost screamed it at me. As a result I felt alienated from them. Some girls think all you need to be beautiful is to be thin. And that's just not true, believe me.

Body Decor

Body art: is it cool or corny? Both, probably. It's very cool when it's in fashion, but corny the moment it becomes yesterday's must-have.

Increasingly we have taken to decorating our bodies. Not just with how we wear our makeup and clothes, but using tattoos and piercings to add to our individuality. Often we can be influenced by music and film stars to decorate ourselves. Trouble is it's more or less accepted practice for rock stars, but it's unlikely to go down well in the more conservative world of, say, IT. So, if you want to experiment with different looks and body art, try out the temporary alternatives—Henna tattoos,

dreads and extensions

Hate your hair? Well, you can change it. Dreads are where you twist your hair into small coils, then leave it to grow. Remember, it takes a while for dreads to reach a length where you can tie them back, and you'll need to say good-bye to conditioning products as they make the dreads fall out. Hair extensions, made from synthetic or human hair fibers, are woven into your own mop. They can look good, but need a lot of care and have to be replaced every so often. Removing them can damage your natural hair, so let a licensed professional do it.

stick-on ones, stick-on body jewels, or body clips that look like piercings. That way when the craze for them is long gone, you can just wash and go on to the next look.

Undeniably tattoos can look very beautiful, when done well. But they are a permanent mark on your skin. Nothing will ever get rid of them. Laser techniques have been developed and

piercing your bits and pieces

Loads of us have pierced ears; some of us have piercings in our nose, lips, belly button, or even our sex organs! The craze for piercings has really taken off in the western world—and if you want to join in, then go for it. Remember, although a pierced hole can close up again there will always be a mark where the hole once was. Piercings can hurt, can get infected, and can go wrong. So be sure you're sure before you go ahead. Always have it done by a licensed professional, and beware of cheap jewelry, which can cause bad skin reactions.

are used to burn the ink off. It can get rid of the tattoo, but tends to leave the skin marked. Washable or henna body art look just as good. If you really want to have a permanent ink one, make sure you use a reputable, licensed tattooist. And maybe choose an area of your body that isn't always on show. That way, if you fall out of love with your art, you can keep it under wraps.

Challenging Nature

Here's some more heavy stuff. It isn't meant to sound like a lecture, but it probably will. Take a deep breath, start reading and stick with it to the very end!

hiding your problems

Remember that surgery isn't the answer to all your problems. It just helps you bury them somewhere else.

What is beauty? Good question. There is no definitive answer because we all see beauty in different ways. Different cultures regard different images as beautiful. This can vary from ample butts or smooth, dark skin, to vivid red hair or stretched necks. There is no one image that is beautiful. So girlies, keep that in mind. Remember that your own beauty comes from your individuality.

Today the world seems to be full of teen girls who are desperately hung up about their looks and are dead-set on changing them. Why? Because we are bombarded with images of unrealistically beautiful celebrities (them again!). Want to know a little secret? The images we see have been carefully doctored; they are not the "real" thing, but society has become so blinkered that it believes in them.

what a beauty you are

No surprise then, that we become obsessed with how we look. Do we look right, look pretty, look hot enough?. Well, guess what? We do. Every single one of us. Because we're individuals. Our skin, hair, eyes, weight, height, everything about us is unique. Don't change that. Just keep yourself aware of the crazy plastic values around you. Don't let yourself be sucked into them and always keep it real. Never judge yourself by the unrealistic media hype of the perceived ideal of beauty. Recognize your own qualities, then flaunt them.

going under the knife

If you hate your nose, breasts, or tummy, medical science enables surgeons to change it; to change you. But know what? Straightening your nose or making your breasts bigger won't change your life. In some circumstances it might make you feel a little more confident, but surgery is not a magical fix-it-all. Being unhappy with the way you look probably has more to do with what's going on inside your head—not on the outside of your body. Never, ever have surgery unless you have had independent counseling from a health professional—that means, don't get counseling from the very person who stands to make money from your surgery.

Breast Augmentation

You've tried being patient while puberty messes around with your breasts, but at the end of it all, you still feel there's room for improvement. What can a girl do?

Melissa, 17

At 15 I had breasts that I hated. They were saggy and looked like they belonged to a grandmother not a teen. I hated them. Whenever I got undressed I felt like crying. I hid my shape in baggy sweaters and longed to have firm breasts. It seemed so unfair that I didn't. Trouble was, I had a kind of warped image of what a normal pair of breasts looked like. I figured they should be a 36, very pert B cup. The summer I was 16 my family went away on vacation to Europe. We were in Spain and the beach was crowded with people, many of them were women who were topless sun-bathing. I was amazed at how different each woman looked! Even young girls my age had such different breasts. Big, small, droopy, upright! It was a revelation to me. I realized I wasn't a freak. Far from it. In fact I was normal. Since then, although I'm still not Miss Confidence-Pants in the breast department, I am much happier with myself. I realized I was comparing myself with people who weren't real.

Terri, 19

By the time I was 17 my breasts were still nonexistent; I wore a 34AA bra. I begged my parents to let me have surgery to fix them but they told me to wait until my 18th birthday. Finally, when I was 19, I had breast augmentation. The surgery went well and I came home with quite fantastic 34B breasts. They were a little too high and hard, but they settled down and they've made a difference. They haven't changed my life, but I feel more confident because I feel I look more normal now.

Leah, 18

My breast implants made me feel fake. From the moment my breasts put in an appearance at the start of puberty, I'd longed for a bigger bust. When it was clear that my breastss weren't going to get any bigger, my Mom bought me a breast augmentation. Trouble was, I hated the attention it brought me. I was quite petite so with a 34D bust I looked top heavy. Guys no longer talked to me—they chatted to my bust. Girls thought I looked trashy. Nightmare. After much consideration, I had them taken out again. I've been left with the scars, but I am happier with the way I look. I think I went into it too hastily. My advice to anyone considering having their breasts changed would be to think about it long and hard. It's no easy option.

Proportions and Portions

The fat club: How many of us, all girls together, sit and moan about how "fat" we are?. Loads of us. Right?

And do you know what? That kinda talk gets sooo dull. We can't change our body type. Through healthy eating and exercise we can alter our shapes a bit, but not hugely. Accept the body type you have. It's what makes you, you. Don't drone on about how much you wish you were different. And you can bet all the imperfections that you can see are lost on your friends and your guy. They love you for you. Not for some idealistic woman you would like to look like. Quit bleating. Get on with your life.

the healthy way to eating healthily

INSTEAD OF "DIETING" EAT HEALTHILY AND TRY TO:

- Eat only when you are hungry, and if you are hungry, eat
- Eat what your body wants, foods from all major groups. Never tell yourself any food is forbidden. Just eat things in moderation.
- Stop eating when you stop feeling hungry

And if you want to feel good about what you're eating, make sure that you include wholesome foods in this. Choose fresh foods, not just pre-packaged, convenience stuff. What could be better than a turkey and cheese sandwich? It's healthy and it's good for you.

Skinny malinky

Yep, the same goes for naturally skinny girls. You have to put up with people accusing you of being anorexic, publicly commenting on your size and shape. If you are naturally thin some people will forever envy that. But skinny girls have just as much body angst. Right? They hate their lack of curves and crave a more womanly shape. Again skinnies just have to accept their shape. Love the skin you're in remember?

healthy eating

As teens we are growing and changing almost by the week. In 12 months we can grow as much as four inches. And all this stretching and developing takes its toll on our body. To help keep it healthy we need to practice "healthy eating" (let's not use the word diet, as diets can be destructive and addictive). Healthy eating means having a good relationship with food and understanding that it is a source of nourishment and development. But lots of us use food for other reasons. Sometimes we eat too much because we're stressed, sad, depressed, or even 'cos we're happy. Sometimes we don't eat for exactly the same reasons. What we have to remember is that to live a healthy life, teens need to eat well. But calorie or carb counting, or any other regulation of our food intake, can lead to an unhealthy attitude to food.

Eating Disorders

Even if you don't think you have a problem with food, please read this section. If it's of no use to you, it might be something you could help a friend with.

triggers of eating disorders

- Problems, or pressure at home, school or both
- Grief at losing a parent, relative, or friend
- Being bullied
- Family upheaval such as divorce or moving house
- Depression
- Physical illness (such as diabetes) putting you under pressure

Experiencing any of these triggers can make you feel insecure, lost, stressed, and alone—and make you turn to food.

Anyone can get an eating disorder. It doesn't mean you're a freak, or ill, or being abused or any of that. Food has become an issue for you, and that's not fine. It's not healthy to live that way. An eating disorder can get to you whether you're black, white, fat, thin, old, or young. It doesn't discriminate. Listen up: as a young woman aged between 15 and 25, you're most at risk.

But you can get better

Really. No matter how desperate you feel or how misunderstood you feel. Step 1 is to figure out why food has taken on this role in your life. That way you can get to the bottom of it all. OK? But don't try to go it alone. There are people who can help you, who understand, who have lived through the same situations as you. There's no magic wand to wave it all away. You must want to get better and to change things about your life. And to make those changes you will be helped all the way. All you need do is ask.

making the first move

Going for help is the very first stage in your recovery. Don't think you will be judged. You won't. The only thing people will think is: great, we're gonna get you better. Believe that you can and will get better. It's not impossible. Starting to get help now is more likely to result in a success than if you ignore your problems.

image isn't everything

It's no thanks to our image-obsessed society that we constantly focus on how we look rather than on how we feel. Feelings are what really count, aren't they? People can get eating disorders when they start to use food as a way of coping with an emotional situation. We're not talking about the occasional chocolate feasts, but a regular pattern of filling our faces with junk food. Before you know it, a diet can lead to a world of binge eating, fasting, vomiting, and starvation. Diet? Don't do it.

Out of Control

Anorexia nervosa

This is when you severely restrict the amount of food you eat. Often, eating disorders are about control. If you feel you're not in control of your life—or even just one area of your life—you start to focus on food, because you can control that, and by controlling food you can control how you look—how much you weigh and the shape of your body. Trouble is when your body is starved of food, your brain is too. And this begins to distort your thinking. So even if your ribs and hips are poking through the skin, an anorexic will

warning signs

- Are you anxious about what you eat?
- Do you prefer to eat in private?
- Do you throw food away when no one's looking?
- Do you lie about what you have eaten?
- Do you comfort eat?
- Have you experienced hair loss?
- Have your normally regular periods become irregular or stopped completely?
- Do you exercise to excess?
- Have you used laxatives to help lose weight?
- Do you make yourself vomit after eating?

still refuse to believe they need to eat. Scary, eh? Long-term effects are reduced fertility and possibly osteoporosis later on. If untreated, anorexia can become so severe that it kills you. Yes, you're thin . . . but you're dead.

tackling disorders from every angle

TREATMENTS FOR EATING DISORDERS INCLUDE:
- Counseling
- Self-help and support groups
- Psychotherapy
- Drama or art therapy
- Therapy sessions that involve the family or small groups of patients
- Diet and nutritional advice

Bulimia nervosa

This is where you binge-eat until you feel so full you will explode, then you make yourself sick, or use laxatives, or both. Sometimes you might get into a rigorous exercise plan to burn off the calories. All in an attempt to prevent weight gain. Bulimia often affects those people who on the outside seem very confident and high achieving. In fact if you have bulimia you probably have low self-esteem and low self-confidence. Controlling your food intake and any weight gain/loss is a way of coping with emotional difficulties.

In a similar way to anorexia, bulimia can take over your life, making you feel trapped and desperate. Chaotic eating and dramatic loss of fluids can cause physical problems, but normal nourishment to the body can usually correct these.

Ready, Set, Go

We all know that exercise is good for you. It keeps you healthy, fit, and toned. But in a society that is increasingly obsessed with fitness, it's easy to get sucked into an exercise plan that is anything but good for you and your body.

put on a good front

Always, always wear a good sports bra, with a strengthened back.

As a rule you should do an aerobic exercise—one that exercises your heart and lungs—three times a week. If you're on a sports team and have to do more, fine. But don't let it take over your life. Like anything else, what starts as a healthy habit can become an unhealthy obsession. If you're at the gym, swimming pool, or aerobics class more often than you're out with your friends, then it's taking over your social life and it's a problem.

So why exercise?

Exercise is good for you. We all hate the fact that we might get hot and sweaty and we jiggle about, but who cares? You keep fit, have fun, make friends. What's bad about that?

Exercise is the best way to keep fit, healthy, and toned. Any exercise is better than none at all—even just walking to school every day. For a balanced program, have a regime of cardiovascular (CV) exercises as well as stretches.

stay in good working order

For the sweatiness, take a shower; for your breasts, wear a good bra. And, no you don't look stupid. You look active, fun, and outgoing. Plus any regular exercise— swimming, tennis, cycling, anything which keeps you coordinated— makes you feel less gangly or awkward and also helps keep your body in good working order and your muscles toned.

something for every body

- For a whole body workout try:
    - Swimming
    - Aerobics
    - Dance
    - Tennis
    - Squash
    - Yoga
    - Pilates
    - Kick-boxing

- For chilling out and stretching try:
    - Low-impact yoga
    - Tai chi

- For the upper arms and back try:
    - Archery
    - Rowing
    - Swimming

- For the legs, thighs and butt try:
    - Horse riding
    - Dance
    - Jogging
    - Biking

And remember that not only is exercise good for you but joining a sports club or exercise class will introduce you to different people and widen your social circle.

Phew ...

So, that's it. Pretty much all the body changes you are likely to go through during your teens. Ready to handle it?

Before you know it you'll be out the other side, even cooler and smarter than ever. How good is that? The main thing you need to know is that all your body changes are pretty normal; they need to happen for you to grow into a gorgeous young woman. Don't be afraid of your new and developing shape. Embrace it. Be happy. Be you.

If you feel freaked out by something, talk it over. Speak to someone about what it is and why you're worried. Your parents or guardians would be a good starting point, but if you can't deal with them, ask your friends. If not them, your healthcare provider. Don't hide from any problem, because that just makes it seem bigger, more scary, and more difficult to deal with. Tackle it head on and get control of it.

Take care of yourself and your body.

And always remember to stay cool.

Joely x

Help is at Hand

TEEN ISSUES

TeenLine:
24-hour, confidential, state-wide, crisis intervention and referral service for teens.
Tel: 1-800-562-1240 or
1-800-722-4222
www.TheTeenLine.org

National Youth Crisis Hotline:
24-hour hotline that provides referrals for teens.
Tel: 1-800-HIT-HOME
(1-800-448-4663)
www.1800hithome.com

SEX AND CONTRACEPTION

Planned Parenthood National Hotline:
24-hour information about contraception and STDs
Tel: 1-800-230-PLAN
(1-800-230-7526)
www.plannedparenthood.org

Not-2-Late:
Directory of doctors, hospitals and family planning clinics that provide emergency contraception.

Tel: 1-888-NOT-2-LATE
(1-888-668-2528)
not-2-late.com at
http://ec.princeton.edu/

PREGNANCY

America's Crisis Pregnancy Hotline:
Confidential information and counseling on pregnancy options.
Tel: 1-888-4-OPTIONS
(1-800-467-8466)
www.thehelpline.org

Teen Pregnancy:
Website of the National Campaign to Prevent Teen Pregnancy
www.teenpregnancy.org

National Abortion Federation
Provides referrals to clinics that perform abortions and answers related questions.
Tel: 1-800-772-9100

STDs

National AIDS Hotline:
Tel: 1-800-342-2437
www.ashastd.org/hotlines/index.
html#stdaids

National STD Hotline:
Confidential information on the treatment and prevention of STDs.
Tel: 1-800-227-8922
www.ashastd.org/hotlines/index.html#stdaids

SEXUAL AND CHILD ABUSE

National Child Abuse Hotline:
Crisis counseling for sexual abuse, domestic violence, rape, and missing children.
Tel: 1-800-422-4453
www.childhelpusa.org

Rape, Abuse, Incest National Network (RAINN):
24-hour hotline
Tel: 1-800-656-HOPE
(1-800-656-4673)
www.rainn.org

EATING DISORDERS

National Eating Disorders Association
Counseling for addressing food and body image issues.
Tel: 1-800-931-2237
www.nationaleatingdisorders.org

DRUG AND ALCOHOL PROBLEMS

National Drug and Alcohol Treatment Hotline:
Tel: 1-800-662-HELP
(1-800-662-4357)

National Drug and Alcohol Treatment Referral Service
Tel: 1-800-662-HELP
(1-800-662-4357)
www.samhsa.gov/csat/

GAY AND LESBIAN

The Trevor Helpline
24-hour, confidential suicide prevention hotline for gay teens.
Tel: 1-800-850-8078

National Gay and Lesbian Hotline:
Counseling services specific to the gay and lesbian community
Tel: 1-888-THE-GLNH
(1-888-843-4564)

SUICIDE

Suicide Hotlines
Tel: 1-800-SUICIDE
(1-800-784-2433)
www.SuicideHotlines.com

Index